BIRD TALES

The Folklore and Natural History of A Few of Our Feathered Friends

By
Brian "Fox" Ellis

**Fox Tales International presents
Fox Tales Folklore**
A Series of Ecological, International
and American Folklore

Other Books in the Fox Tales Folklore Series :
A River of Stories
Tall Tree Tales
Fox Tales
Fish Tales
Fun with Fables
Celtic Tales
River Ghosts
Prairie Tales
Speaking Truth to Power
In A Spring Garden

*Each book in the series is available as an ebook, paperback
audio-book, podcast and video!*

*Please contact Fox for wholesale orders,
library and school discounts.*

*Cover art, book design, and interior illustrations
by Devin McSherry.
www.devinmcsherry.com*

Fox Tales International

Presents

BIRD TALES

The Folklore and Natural History of
A Few of Our Feathered Friends

**Researched, Written, Edited and Performed
by Brian "Fox" Ellis**

Copyright © 2020 Brian "Fox" Ellis
All Rights Reserved
ISBN # 9798650582861

Fox Tales International
P.O. Box 209
Bishop Hill, IL 61419
www.foxtalesint.com

BIRD TALES
by Brian "Fox" Ellis

Table of Contents

The Sun's Symphony 1
How Birds Got Their Feathers 2
The Squirrel and the Thrush... 7
Hummingbird Places the Stars 8
Hummingbird's Ruby Throat 11
Hummingbird and Crane 14
The Lord of the Cranes 18
The Crane Maiden 22
The Whooping Cranes' Migration 28
Crane Poetry 33
The Wise Quail 34
Jumping Mouse 36
The Bittern and the Mussel 49
Snow Buntings' Lullaby...50
Meadowlark..53
Write Your Own Bird Tales 54

THE SUN'S SYMPHONY

I love the morning symphony
when a distant lark begins to sing
and behind you in a bush
a musical trill rises up
with the growing light.
Another bird joins in, a wren
a warbler, too, robin and thrush.
Until soon there are a hundred voices
singing a dozen songs.

And all along this longitude
from snowy tundra to mountain forest,
sage desert to tall grass prairie,
coastal swamp to island reef,
the choir draws an invisible line.

Wherever the sun touches the earth anew,
a new song rises up
to greet this new day.

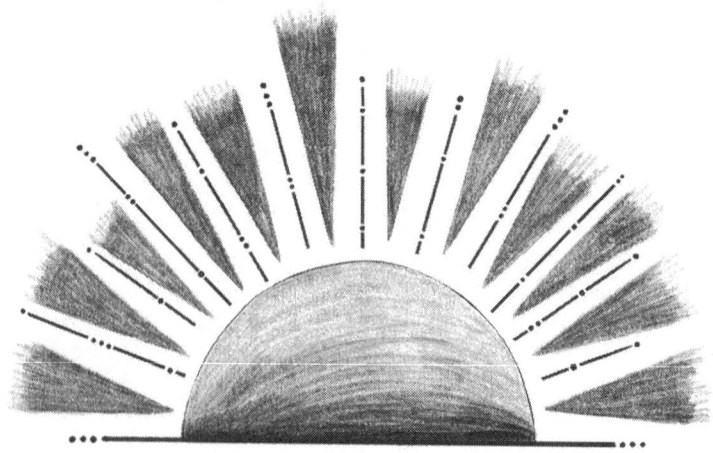

HOW BIRDS GOT THEIR FEATHERS
A Traditional Iroquois Story

In the beginning when the world was new, there were a few things that were left undone. For one thing, the birds had no feathers. Whenever it was cold and wet the birds would huddle together to keep each other warm, but it was never enough. When it was hot and sunny the birds got sunburned all over their bodies. Our Creator looked down and took pity on the birds. One night, Creator sent all of the birds a dream. That night all of the birds had the same dream. In the morning, when the birds awoke, they began to talk.

"Last night I had the strangest dream!"
"No!"
"Yeah!"
"I had the same dream!"
"No?"
"Yeah!"

So all of the birds gathered in a large circle, because Native people believe, as I believe, that we all have a good mind. And when we put our minds together, we come up with the best ideas. So everyone was listened to, everyone was given that respect. A little bird flew forward and said, *"Last night I had the strangest dream. I dreamed that Creator called one of us to the sky world to be the messenger for all of the birds. There was a long-house filled with suits of feathers, all of the colors of the rainbow. And one of us should fly to the sky world to bring those feathers back."*

The birds looked around. Who would be the messenger for all of the birds?

First they looked at Eagle. He had long wings. He could fly higher than almost any bird. He was the chief of the bird tribe

But Eagle said, *"No. I am the chief of the bird tribe. I should stay here and watch over my flock. One of you should be the messenger for all of the birds."*

The birds looked around. Next they looked at Vulture.

"Vulture, your wings are nearly as long as Eagle's. We have seen you fly as high as Eagle. You should do it."

"No..." said Vulture, *"I, I, I couldn't do that. Find, find someone else."*

"Please," said the other birds, *"We need you."*

"No, I, I don't think I could, I couldn't do anything like that..."

"Please, we have seen you fly for hours hardly flapping at all. We need you."

Because they had faith in her, somehow, she found a little faith in herself. *"All, Alright, I'll try."*

Vulture spread her long wings and began to soar, in large circles, higher and higher... but she had not had a good breakfast. She ran out of food, she ran out of fuel. She could not do it. Just then she smelled a dead rotten catfish along the shore of a river. She was really, really hungry. Vulture found that when she peeled back the skin, inside here was still some good meat she could eat. She filled her belly. And ever since that time vultures have a had a taste for things long dead. With food she had fuel. She spread her wings and began to fly, higher and higher, in large circles she flew. Higher and higher, she flew higher than she had ever flown before. She flew so close to the sun that her head was burned red. That is why, still too this day, the Turkey Vulture has a red head. She flew to the sky world!

Creator said, "Vulture, you are the messenger for all of the birds. Come with me." Just like in their dreams, there was a long-house filled with suits of feathers, all of the colors of the rainbow. Creator said, *"Since you are the messenger for all of the birds you get first choice, any suit of feathers you like. But one thing you must not forget: If you try on a suit of feathers and then give it away you cannot put it on again."*

No problem, thought Vulture. (Listen as I will tell you what the suit of feathers looked like and you see if you can guess who it was given to before I say their name.) The first suit of feathers was a dark slate grey, almost black, except it had a red vest. But that red vest made her belly look big and she did not like that, so she gave it to... yes, Robin Red Breast. The next suit of feathers was a bright yellow, so bright you might call it gold. And it had really cool black wings, with a white stripe, like a racing stripe. She tried this on, but it also had a black cap that was too small, so she took this one off and gave it to... yes, goldfinch!

The next one was a rich deep dark chocolate brown, so dark it was also almost black, but it came with a white tail and a white hat. The white hat made her look bald. She didn't like that so she gave this suit of feathers to ... eagle, bald eagle! Suit after suit she gave away. None of them were good enough for the messenger of all of the birds. (Let's try a harder one...)

The next suit of feathers was a brilliant blend of black and a bright fiery orange and red. There were black and white wings with a red-orange throat, a small bit of a black eye stripe and a black triangle on the cheek, and a black and orange striped hat, but that hat... she didn't like that, so she gave it away to... (any guesses?) If you said the Blackburnian warbler you really know your birds! Suit after suit she gave away. Until finally, she had given them all away!

She went back to the longhouse and it was empty... uh... oh... umm... she thought it was empty. There was one suit of feathers left. It was on the dirt floor and the color of dirt so she did not see it at first. Yuck, it smelled bad. But she had tried on every other suit, so she tried on this one, too. It didn't fit at all. The pants were too short so her bare legs stuck out down below. It had no hat, so her bright red head stuck out the top. She tried to take it off… ugh… Ugh… UGH! But it was stuck. It would not come off.

Creator said, *"Vulture, you have given away every other suit. That is the last one. You are stuck with that suit for the rest of your days."*

Oh, she was so disappointed. She could have been any color she wanted, but now she was stuck with this ugly, smelly, dirty old thing! She flew down to the earth. She hid in an ancient oak tree. She looked out from the tree and she saw the red of robin, the blue of blue jay, the gold of goldfinch. And do you know why they were flying around? They were looking for Vulture, so they could say thank you.

Robin found her. Robin shouted, *"Over here! Over here! Over here!"* And all of the birds flew into that tree.

Now let us pause for moment and imagine that tree. Can you imagine the largest old oak tree and there are birds on every branch! Every bird you can imagine, every color of the rainbow.

When all of the birds gathered, Vulture said, *"Go Away! Leave me alone!"* (Have you ever heard this before? Have you ever said this before? Does this person really want to be left alone? Sometimes, but usually they are crying for attention.)

Robin said, *"Vulture, what's wrong?"*

"I don't want to talk about it…" Vulture sobbed.

"Oh, you can tell me," soothed Robin.

"I don't want to talk about it …" Vulture sobbed, *"Go Away!"*

But Robin noticed. Vulture would look at her feathers and then look at the other birds, look at her feathers and look at Robin's red breast, look at her feathers and then gaze longingly at the brilliant blue of Indigo Bunting.

Robin asked, *"Is it your feathers? Is that what's bothering you?"*

Vulture nodded.

"Oh, Vulture, you should know," said Robin, *"it does not matter what you wear, what color your clothes, or skin, it's what's inside that matters…"*

Vulture felt a little better. She stopped sobbing, took a deep breathe, and looked around at the gratitude in the eyes of all of her friends… she thought about it… she did have a reason to be proud. She was after all the messenger for all of the birds!

And that is how that story goes, Ho! Hey!

THE SQUIRREL AND THE THRUSH
A Russian Fable

Once there was a wealthy man who gave his children whatever they wanted. His son wanted a squirrel, so he hired a woodcutter to capture a squirrel. They purchased a huge gilded cage with a large wheel so the squirrel could get his exercise. Every day the squirrel spent hours running, running, running but never getting anywhere. The wheel hummed with his effort.

The cage was placed near a window, so the squirrel could look out into the forest that was once his home. An old friend of the squirrel, a wood thrush, would sometimes come and sit on a branch outside the window and sing her glorious trills.

One day the thrush asked the squirrel, *"What are you doing inside that cage?"*

"I am a messenger for a busy and important merchant. There are notes to deliver, packages to receive, and letters to send," replied the squirrel, *"I am running, running, running in order to get everything done!"*

"Yes, it is obvious that you are running," sang the thrush, *"But why do you scurry so fast without getting anywhere? Though you are always moving, you are always in the same place."*

To this, the squirrel had no reply. He kept on running because that was what he did. As for the thrush, she flew off to the dark heart of the forest, where her song can still be heard by those who take the time to listen.

HUMMINGBIRD PLACES THE STARS
An Old Campfire Story

In the beginning, when the world was new, there were a few things left undone. In this beginning time, it was always daylight. There was no night. All of the animals were up and about eating and being eaten. But some animals grew really tired of eating and others grew really tired of being eaten! And the things being eaten were soon to disappear. Soon there would be nothing left to eat. When everything was gobbled up the creatures of this world would starve. It was out of balance. Our world was out of balance. Our Creator decided this would not do and had to do something. We all needed a time to rest. So Creator threw a huge wet blanket over the entire world just to slow things down. But it was so dark, no one could see where they were going! BANG! Cougar ran into a tree! AHH! Bear fell off a cliff! SO all of the animals, calling out for help, slowly found each other, and gathered into a large circle. I believe, and maybe you would agree? We all have a good mind, when we use it. And if we put our minds together we come up with the best ideas. SO everyone should be listened to, everyone should be respected.

The animals discussed many things, until finally, someone said, *"Eagle, you can fly higher than almost any other bird. You should fly up there and see what it is that is blocking out the sun."* Everyone agreed. Because it was so dark, no one could see, little tiny hummingbird wanted to help, to do her part, so little tiny hummingbird slipped into the feathers of the eagle. A hummingbird weighs less than a nickel, so the eagle did not notice.

Eagle began to fly, in large circles, higher and higher, until UGH! Eagle ran into that wet blanket. He turned and grabbed a huge chunk of blanket and ripped it out with his large talons. In that very moment a large circle of light was cast down upon the earth. The animals could see! All of the animals cheered! Eagle turned and headed back down towards the earth.

What the animals down below did not see, at first, was this: at the very moment the eagle turned to fly down, Hummingbird slipped out of his feathers. She fluttered around and began poking at the blanket. Because Hummingbird is the only bird who can fly backwards and upside down, she used her long narrow beak to poke hole after hole in that big old wet blanket.

At first it might have seemed random, but then she began to outline pictures of all of her friends down below, bear and swan, crab and cougar. As the light grew a little brighter and a little brighter, some of the animals noticed. They told their friends to look up and soon everyone saw it. As hummingbird drew picture after picture the animals down below began to cheer, again and again, especially when they recognized themselves in the pictures!

Our Creator looked on and seeing the animals working together, cheering together, Creator smiled. Hoping maybe the animals had learned something, it was left this way. That large round hole slowly heals itself each month and grows smaller, until it is a dark night, then it grows larger until it is a bright light, we call the moon.

The moon is there in phases, to remind us of the balance we all need, so those who hunt at night can see where they are going, and it gets dark sometimes so those who are eaten have a chance to hide. But the stars are always there so there is at least some light on the darkest night. You can look up there tonight and see all of the animals dancing together. That light is always there, to remind of this story, to remind us of hummingbird. Those little lights are still there, even on a dark night, so we can always find our way home, home back to our kith and kin.

HUMMINGBIRD'S RUBY THROAT
A South American Por Que' or How and Why Story

Today we think of the hummingbird as one of the most gorgeous birds, iridescent colors glowing in the sunlight, but it wasn't always so. Many long years ago, the hummingbird was a rather plain looking bird, mousy grey, drab. This is the story of how the hummingbird earned those brilliant colors.

It was a hot and steamy morning in the rainforest, so the hummingbird was resting on a small branch above a commonly used trail, just watching the world go by. Just then he saw a huge buck, a huge deer came bounding down the trail with panic in his eyes. Hummingbird quickly saw why. The deer was being chased by a sleek panther. The deer leapt a fallen log and seems to disappear as quick as it appeared. The panther was so intent on catching its breakfast that she did not notice, when she jumped over the log her huge paw went splat and smashed a small mouse nest with several blind baby mice inside it. The panther kept running after the deer, unaware of the mother mouse and her babies.

The mother mouse was angry! Infuriated! She immediately began to scold the panther, *"Who do you think you are smashing my nest! You should watch where you are going! I will teach you to mess with a mother mouse!"* And on she went chasing the cat.

Now imagine this scene, a deer running down the trail, chased by a large cat, chased by a little tiny mouse! *"You come back here right now!"* shouted the little mouse. The hummingbird thought this was hilarious! He thought he would follow this little parade to see what might become of this game of chase. The deer had disappeared. Most large cats fail about 6 out of 7 times, or maybe we should say they succeed one out of seven times because they never give up! The panther was exhausted with the chase. She decided to rest by the side of a small stream. Soon the panther was asleep and slept through the long heat of the day. She would try to hunt again in the cool of the evening. Because the panther stopped, the mouse was eventually able to catch up. Still scolding the panther, the mouse said, *"I will teach you a lesson, to watch where you are going!"* She went down to the edge of the stream and scooped up a small bit of soft clay mud. She placed the mud on the eyes of the panther. Scoop after scoop of soft clay mud she gently placed all around and onto the eyes of this sleeping cat. *"There! That ought to teach you! Not watching where you are going? You will not see anything ever again!"* said the mother mouse. Then she scampered away.

The hummingbird saw it all. And he saw something no one else saw. As the sun rose over the trees, the soft clay began to bake. As the sun dried the clay, it turned to stone. Soon the clay was baked by the sun and as hard as a rock. The hummingbird laughed. This ought to be good, he thought. He decided to find a perch and wait to see what came next.

When the panther woke up, just before sunset, she stretched her face and tried, Tried, TRIED to open her eyes. They would not open! She stumbled about! Blind! BOOM! She ran into a tree. Splash! She fell into the stream! She screamed! She roared! The hummingbird laughed and laughed before taking pity on the panther.

He flew down and buzzed around the panthers face. *"Be still. I think I can help,"* said the hummingbird. As the hummingbird used its long, strong beak to slowly peck and chip away at the clay, the hummingbird told the panther what had just happened.

The panther opened its eyes. It saw the hummingbird for the first time. *"Thank you, thank you, for what you have done. I see the world like I have never seen it before!"* said the panther. *"Is there some way I can repay you?"*

"No," said the hummingbird, *"this has been an entertaining day and I am happy to help."*

"Please," said the panther, *"allow me to do something. I know. Since you are so plain and grey, allow me to bring beauty to your world as you have brought sight to mine!"* The panther chewed some soft green leaves and then rubbed the juice on the hummingbird's back. It then reached down into the mud and pulled out some bright red clay with flecks of mica, a shiny, glittery mineral, and rubbed this on the hummingbirds throat. *"It is the least I can do for your kindness,"* said the panther.

And so it was, and so it is still to this day: if you see a ruby-throated hummingbird with it's brilliant emerald green back and its bright red ruby throat you now know how it got those colors. And those colors are still there, to remind of this story, to remind us, that one good deed, indeed deserves another.

HUMMINGBIRD AND CRANE
A Traditional Cherokee Story

She was hot! She was a long, tall, cool drink of water and one look at her made you thirsty! Part of her charm was that she was also clever; she exuded strength and confidence in the way she walked, the way she noticed you notice her and gave you a wink, just to pique your interest. She was the kind of woman who knew what she wanted and knew how to get it. She would not settle for second best.

Most of the birds knew she was out of their league and did not even try. Most birds found someone of their temperament, their temperature, and were happy to day dream, happy to settle down with a good woman who knew how to be good to them. The suitors, one by one faded away.

Oh, she had trouble deciding. The two who showed the most interest in her, the two who would not give up, were Whooping Crane and Hummingbird.

Whooping Crane was gawky. He was tall and lanky, awkward, with big feet and a big heart. He was also a great dancer. In the council circle, on the powwow grounds, all of his angular limbs seemed to melt into waving grasses. WHOOP! WHOOP! WHOOP! He was an amazing, fancy dancer. She also knew he was a great hunter. He could catch frogs and snakes like nobody's business.

But Hummingbird, Ruby Throated Hummingbird, oh, he was a whole 'nother matter. He was handsome, with his ruby red throat, his emerald green back and his buff white chest. She was reluctant to admit it, but he was almost as gorgeous as she was… *(What? She was just admitting what everyone knew.)* He was also fast! He could zip around here and there and be back in an instant, with an insect, he had just caught and coated in nectar for a sweet tasty treat. He was always bringing her presents. Humpf, she had trouble deciding?

So one evening at the council circle, she announced to all who were listening that there would be a race: a race to the distant mountains and back and whoever won would be her man. She would let them decide, though of course she was hoping it would be Hummingbird who won. He was fast.

The next morning, all of the bird tribe gathered at the council grounds in the center of the village. Hummingbird rested on a twig. Whooping Crane just stood there flat-footed. As the signal was given, Hummingbird zipped up, flew once around the crowd for sport and then disappeared. Everyone cheered!

Whooping Crane took a few awkward steps, flapped his wings and began flying off... in the wrong direction! The others tried not to laugh. He began making big circles. Other birds wondered if he knew which way to go, but he knew what he was doing. He was looking for a thermal, a place where the sun had begun to warm the earth. The warm air would lift him higher and higher. Soon he appeared to be smaller than hummingbird. He disappeared into the clouds. Other birds shook their heads and wondered how far ahead Hummingbird must be by now.

But those who knew Crane knew he had the greatest stamina and endurance; no, not the fastest bird, but he could fly all night - and that is what he did.

Hummingbird stopped near dusk. He fed on a few flowers and munched a few insects to keep his strength up. He had been to the mountains before and figured it would take six or seven days. In the morning, he fed again. Shortly after he zipped off towards the mountains, he was shocked to find Crane wading in a stream catching fish for his breakfast. How had Crane caught up!? Hummingbird pushed himself and flew faster and further than he had ever flown before.

Crane just smiled and nodded as Hummingbird flew past. After a little rest he found another thermal and let the warmth of the earth lift him up; from this height he could glide for miles with hardly a flap, saving his strength for the long night.

The next morning, Hummingbird flew for some time without seeing any sign of Crane. Mid-morning, could you imagine his surprise, when he found that Crane was finishing his breakfast and already looking for a sun-warmed meadow?

And so it went each day, Crane was a little further ahead. Hummingbird kept passing him, but each day it was later in the day. On the fourth day, as Hummingbird approached the top of the sacred mountain, above the village of Katuah, he passed Crane, who was already on his way home!

On the fifth day, Hummingbird passed Crane near supper time. On the sixth day, he did not see Crane at all. He became frantic. On the seventh day, Crane did take a little rest; he bathed and groomed himself in the stream nearest his village. He came into the council grounds well before the sun reached its apex.

The whole village was there waiting. Most were surprised, except those who knew Crane. Most said he looked handsome, regal even, but no one said anything about the disappointment in her eyes. Hummingbird came into the council circle late in the evening, just before sunset, and he looked bedraggled, beaten and confused.

And so her choice was made, or was it?

Though she did not marry him, she never married, she became a medicine woman so she could share her love and wisdom with the entire village, but she did whisper something into Whooping Crane's ear. And though he never told it, it made him blush, the whole top of his head turned beet red. You see those are not red feathers on Crane's head, that is skin. And just as you turn red when you blush, so does Crane.

Years later when he was an old bird, happily married to another bird of his kind, he always smiled when he remembered that day… and then he would look at his wife, and she would blush like a young hen when he looked at her that way.

THE LORD OF THE CRANES
A Taoist Folktale

High in the mountains of China, near the Tibetan border, there was an old Taoist monastery. At one time it was a large school for Taoist thought, but as the earth spun around the sun again and again, eventually there was just one old man living there. He had spent his entire life here. He was quite content with the quiet life this mountain retreat brought to him. Here, he was attuned to the cycles of life and the cycles of the season. Some thought him one of the immortals. All who knew him, knew him as an honored elder.

Every autumn, about the time he harvested his rice from the fields, he would listen for the song of the cranes. The high pitched WHOOP and tremulous PURR would send a shiver of joy down his spine. These cranes are among the highest flying of all the birds, flying to heaven in their annual migration over the tallest mountains in the world, reaching heights of 25,000 feet above sea level. The old man would go down into his rice paddies and dance and sing with the cranes. He would play his flute and the cranes would dance with him. He was known as the Lord of the Cranes.

The cranes would spend several days feasting and resting before continuing their long migration. When the cranes left, the old man would make his annual pilgrimage into the village far below his mountain retreat. Once a year, he would go to market, beg for a few coins, hoping to raise enough money to buy the few things he could not grow or make for himself. But this year, the people were not kind, they were not generous. Some were rude to him and even worse, some ignored him like he was not even there, somehow, less than human.

The old man stood on a street corner near the market place for most of the day. Across the street was a small inn and place for most of the day. Across the street was a small inn and restaurant. During the lull in afternoon business, the innkeeper liked to sit on a bench in front of his shop and watch the hustle and bustle of the marketplace. That afternoon he watched the old man with some curiosity. At first he was enchanted by the old man's movements, spry and agile for his age, his wry smile, and the way he was kind to everyone who passed. Then the innkeeper was appalled, angry at the way people treated the old man, harsh and rude. The innkeeper called out, *"Hey, kind sir, would you honor me by joining me for a cup of tea?"*

The old man was happy to be invited, but warned, *"I have no money. I cannot pay for any tea."*

The innkeeper said, *"I will not let you pay, you are a guest, and an honored guest at that."*

As the two settled into a booth, the innkeeper motioned to his waiter to bring food. After tea was served, plate after plate arrived laden with the best noodles, tender stuffed dumplings in broth, rich sauces, rice with cabbage and pickles, and sweets for dessert. The afternoon quickly passed into evening. Customers slowly began filling the restaurant.

The old man stood up. He stretched. He said, "Please let me repay your kindness with a kindness of my own."

At first the innkeeper was ready to protest, but before he could say anything, the old man did an unusual thing. He pulled out a long crane feather that was tied to the top of his walking stick. He dipped it into a gourd filled with water and he began to paint, with water he painted a large empty wall within the inn. The old man's movement was graceful, an elegant dance. As he brushed the wall with his crane feather colors appeared. The old man danced and flapped his arms, painting the movements of cranes. He rose up and bowed down painting the mountains, rising and falling into the distance. He twirled and flowed across the wall painting the current of the river. He seemed to float up off the floor as he painted the rising clouds. By now everyone in the restaurant was watching. They saw this vacant wall soon filled with the most beautiful image of mountains and a river, flying clouds and dancing cranes.

The innkeeper said, *"This is the most beautiful painting I have ever seen."*

"Oh, but I am not yet done," said the old man, pulling a small bamboo flute from his waistband. He clapped three times and began to play his flute. The crowd began to clap along. The cranes painted on the wall began to leap up and to dance to everyone's delight. When he was done, he clapped three times and the cranes were back on the wall. *"Every night, when the inn is busy, clap three times and play a flute and the cranes will dance for you. Clap three times when they are done and they will be mere paintings once again,"* said the old man. And he left.

As you could imagine, word swiftly spread about the dancing cranes. Soon the restaurant was busier than it had ever been before. People travelled far and wide to visit the inn, to see the cranes. They came back again and again because the food was great and most importantly, it was served with kindness. The next night and every night, the innkeeper kept the one booth open, hoping his friend would return. When the evening was late and he did not see the old man, he would invite other needful people and share a free meal with them. Word of this kindness also spread.

When the year had passed, after the rice had been harvested, and the cranes had begun their migration south, the old man returned to the village. The innkeeper rushed over as soon as he saw the old man. He invited him to his restaurant and ordered a feast to be spread. He told the old man all about the glorious year he had and how much his business had grown. *"And I owe it all to you! Here, I have saved a few coins and I want to share this joy with you."*

The old man humbly accepted the gift. He could feel from the weight of the purse he would not be hungry any time soon. But after the meal was eaten and the crowd had thinned out for the night, the old man rose, clapped three times and played his flute. The cranes leapt off the wall, but the paintings were still there. The old man said, *"I am glad my cranes could help you, but they must migrate south with their families. It is time for us to go."*

"Thank you, thank you, thank you ten thousand times," said the innkeeper, *"How could I ever repay you for what you have done?"*

The old man said, *"Repay me with your continued kindness to strangers. Make sure there is always one seat in your restaurant for the hungry."* And then the old man climbed onto the back of a crane. They flew off towards the mountains. They disappeared into the clouds.

The innkeeper knew he had been blessed. And though the cranes on the wall would no longer dance like they once did, the reputation of the innkeeper and his kindness would last. The business would flourish. And people would still come to see the portrait of the dancing cranes. When the music would play, everyone would dance. And still to this day, in the autumn, when the people hear the high pitch WHOOP and tremulous PURR of the cranes, their eyes and hearts turn heavenward.

THE CRANE MAIDEN
A Japanese Folktale

High in the mountains of Japan there lived an old woodcutter and his wife. They lived a simple life. Every morning he would go into the forest and cut down a few old trees, lop off their branches, bundle the wood onto his back and take it to the marketplace to sell or trade for the few things he and his wife would need. Sometimes he would slowly burn the wood and bury the fire to make charcoal, which he could sell for a little more when they needed it. He knew his way around the forest and seemed to know when and where to cut trees so there would always be more trees in the future. He thinned the young trees that grew too close together. He harvested the old trees to make room for the new. And he planted a few trees each spring for the ones he had cut down the winter before.

One cold winter day, he was higher in the mountains than he would usually travel. He saw huge storm clouds begin to gather in the distance. He quickly bundled up his wood as the snow began to blow. As he settled his bundle on his back for the long journey home, he heard an unsettling cry from deep in the forest. It was the most mournful high pitched hoop. He recognized the call of the crane, but it was the saddest and most heartfelt wailing he had ever heard. It was not flying overhead as one would expect. It sounded like it was coming from the ground, stationary.

He set down his bundle of wood. He headed towards the direction where the cry was coming from. Because of the snow white feathers of the crane, at first he saw just the red cap and black neck. When it flapped its wings he saw the black wing tips. Then he noticed the crane was caught in a trap that must have been set for some small rodent. He knew cranes will sometimes eat rodents, but in order for the crane to be caught, it must have been hungry and desperate to go for the bait.

The old woodcutter spoke soothingly to the crane as he slowly moved towards the frightened bird. The young crane calmed at the old man's gentle touch. The old man struggled to release the trap from the crane's leg. He could see a little blood, but he also felt that the leg was not broken. The skin was rubbed raw with the bird's struggle to get free. When the crane was released from the trap, it stretched its legs, walked in a circle around the old woodcutter and then stretched its wings. Before it flew off it looked into his eyes. That look, that look of deep gratitude was all the thanks the woodcutter would ever need. In the distance he heard the cry of a crane, a cry of gratitude. He saw a snow white crane circling and circling, higher and higher, until it too disappeared in the snowy clouds.

The old man headed back towards his bundle of wood. He put the bundle on his back. He headed down the mountainside. When he returned home his wife was at first worried about him. But when he told her the story of the crane, she hugged him and said, *"This kindness is why I married you. And it is why I still love you these many years later."* They ate a simple dinner and settled in for a long cold night of sleep. Because he knew the labor that went into cutting wood and making charcoal, they were always frugal about how much they burned to warm their small home.

No sooner were they asleep, when they were startled to hear someone knocking on their door. *"Who could it be on this cold and snowy night?"* He sprang from the bed and opened the door to see a young woman wearing a tattered white kimono with black and red embroidery. *"Come in, come in,"* insisted the old man, *"Come in out of the cold. Why are you traveling in the mountains on such a cold night?"*

They ushered the girl to the fireplace. They wrapped her in blankets and gave her tea to chase away the cold. When she stopped shivering she explained that she had no family, well, she was on her way to an auntie's house on the other side of the mountain, an auntie she barely remembered from when she was a little girl. She was hoping the auntie would take her in.

The elderly couple insisted that she stay with them for the night. It was too late and too cold to travel over the mountains. They shared a humble meal and made more tea for her. They made her a bed by the fire. Everyone was soon asleep.

When the woodcutter and his wife awoke in the morning, their young guest had already cleaned their small home, rekindled the fire and made tea. She made porridge for them. She gladly helped with the chores and did most of the work to prepare dinner and wash up after. She spent a second night in their home since it continued to snow outside. The winter snows lasted for several days. The girl stayed. Days became weeks and weeks became months. When the snow finally melted in the mountains and the spring flowers began to bloom, the young woman began to help in the garden. She seemed to be a friend to every child in the neighborhood. She brought such warmth and delight to the old couple.

In passing conversation, the girl hinted that she did not know this auntie of hers very well. She was not even sure if she would be welcome in her home. This made the old woman and the woodcutter very happy. They had been whispering at night in bed, wondering if the girl would stay. She was such a delight, the child they never had. This decided it. The next day they asked the girl to stay, not as a servant, but as the daughter they always wished to have. The girl said yes. That night while whispering in bed the old man said to his wife, *"How I wish I had a few extra coins to buy our new daughter a new silk kimono for the New Year."* The young girl heard this wish.

The next morning she said she had a present for the older couple, a way of thanking them for welcoming her into their home when she had none. She had noticed a spinning wheel and a loom in storage. She asked that it be set up in the back room and she be left alone for four days. *"Please, whatever you do, do not look, do not take even one peek. In four days I will show what I have done."*

They granted her wish. Though they saw no silk or cotton or material of any kind, they soon heard the whirl, whirl, whirl of the spinning wheel. They heard the clack-tika-tika, clack-tika-tika of the loom. It seemed to never stop. For four days and nights the girl worked undisturbed in the back room. At the end of the forth day she came out. Looking bedraggled and tired, she held the most beautiful snow white silk. A large bolt of cloth that seemed so pure and white that it glowed with a light from within. Though it was white on white, there was a pattern of shimmering cranes dancing in the intricate embroidery and weaving.

She said to her father, *"Please do not sell this fabric. Take it to the marketplace and people will offer you money, more than you would ask for, accept whatever they offer as a gift and give them the cloth."* This was a strange request, but he did what was asked of him. Even before he got to the marketplace people began to admire the fabric. They had seen nothing like it! Soon a small crowd had gathered.

Someone said, *"I will give you five coins of silver for such cloth."*
"Five! I will give you ten!
"Silver! I will give you ten coins of gold!" said another.
"Ten? I will give you twenty coins!"
"Twenty five"
"Thirty!"
"Fifty!"

And so it went. The old man asked for nothing, but graciously accepted what was offered, much more than he would have dreamed of, let alone requested. The old man bought his daughter a beautiful kimono and another for his wife. He bought fresh fish for sushi and rice candy for a treat. And he still had a purse filled with coins, gold coins!

They lived quite well for quite a while, but when you have money, you spend money. It was not long before the money ran out. The woodcutter and his wife asked if she could weave some more of the magical cloth. Winter was once again on its way and they could use the money to make the winter more bearable. This time they promised they would be more frugal.

"No, I cannot," said the girl, *"it is very difficult for me and it is too soon."*

They hinted. They pleaded. They asked again, and the girl gave in.

"Once more you must leave me alone for four days and nights. Please do not look in on me," she asked.

When the neighbors heard the whirl, whirl, whirl of the spinning wheel they knew what was happening in the woodcutter's home. When they heard the clack-tika-tika, clack-tika-tika, they knew the girl was weaving the magical cloth. It is hard to keep a secret in a small village. Soon the neighbors were asking, *"Where does she get her material to spin and weave?"*

"Are you not worried about your daughter, alone, without food and water for four days?"

"She is your daughter, no? How is it that she can tell you what you can and cannot do?"

The old couple tried to ignore these questions. They tried to kindly brush away the neighbors and their questions, but one neighbor asked, *"Are you not at least a little bit curious? Are you not a little bit worried? Would it really hurt if you just peeked a little bit, to make sure she was alright?"*

The mother gave in to her curiosity and concern. She slid the rice paper door open just a sliver to take a small peek. What she saw stunned her! She shut the door quickly, but the girl heard the door and looked up in time. The mother saw not a girl, but a snow white crane. She was plucking her own feathers, bleeding from a thousand small wounds. She was spinning and weaving the feathers into a fine fabric. The old woman wept, but said nothing. A few moments later the girl emerged holding a nearly complete bolt of cloth, just as beautiful as before, but this time each embroidered crane had a red crown, a drop of blood, a stain, so carefully placed it made the head of the crane stand out in the snow white field. *"Again, you must not sell this cloth, simply accept what is offered,"* the girl said, *"but now that you know my true nature I cannot stay with you. I thank you for your many acts of kindness, and most especially for freeing me. You saved my life. I wish there was more I could give to you. But I must go."* She walked away into the woods. A gentle snow began to fall as she disappeared in the forest. In the distance they heard the cry of a crane, a cry of gratitude. They saw a snow white crane circling and circling, higher and higher, until it too disappeared in the snowy clouds.

The money they received from this partial bolt of cloth was enough for them to make it through the winter and well into the following spring. They grew old together enjoying their simple life. But every winter, when the first snows began to fly, they would listen for the migrating cranes. Every year one crane would circle low and cry out, a high pitched whoop and a tremulous purr of gratitude. The old couple would embrace, and shed a tear for what might have been... A crane maiden to call their own.

THE WHOOPING CRANES' MIGRATION
A True Science Tale

At first light, a crane lifts its long legs, stretches its wings, WHOOP, WHOOP, WHOOP! It seems to be singing up the sun!

Cranes dance! Their Red head and long tail feathers give them the Appearance of a fancy dancer to rival the Lakota. Nearer and nearer his mate, clacking beaks together, soon they are Entangled in the dance of love.

These cranes will bond for life.

Look, now, the male and female are working together to build a nest of cattails, sedges, bulrushes and other aquatic plants. The mound of vegetation slowly takes shape here in a swampy estuary where their young are free from harm. The mother lays her eggs and both parents take turns warming them, protecting them. The mother bird plucks a few feathers from her breast. In this way she can line the nest with the insulation of her feathers and her bare skin touches the eggs so more of her warmth incubates them.

Four weeks pass.

Do you see the eggs begin to stir? They wriggle. A small crack appears. The egg tooth emerges first; this special bump on the beak of the baby bird helps it to crack the egg. Their feathers are wet with albumen. Two chicks emerge from their eggs. The mother keeps them warm, hidden beneath her wings.

The father brings snacks, small fish, tadpoles, and insects, all partially digested by his stomach acids. He regurgitates the food into their hungry beaks. These first few weeks are the most precarious. A red fox has been seen hunting the shore line of the swamp. Hawks by day, owls by night prowl the sky. The parents are ever diligent watching over their young.

The long legged babies slowly lose their newborn fluff. Dirty beige flight feathers begin to grow. Three more weeks pass before they begin dancing and flapping, stretching their wing muscles in preparation for flight. The parents lead them on a parade through the cattails and along the edges of the swamp. They are looking for anything that moves!

See the parents gobble up small snakes, large crawfish, fish, mice, frogs and toads, almost anything they can catch. For the first few weeks the parents then turn and share their food with these two awkward chicks, but as they grow taller and more agile the teenage whooping cranes begin snatching up beetles and grasshoppers, slugs and snails. Watching their parents, they learn what is good to eat and more important, how to catch it!

Now nearly as tall as their parents, the young cranes begin whooping, leaping, dancing and stretching for the clouds. They watch their parents fly and yearn to join them in the sky. Because of their weight, their long legs and wings, the crane must get a running start. They begin to flap as they run and a strong gust coming across the field lifts them into the air. Can you feel the joy they must feel as they take their first flight?

This first flight leads to many more. Though more graceful than a pterodactyl, they share the same ancient affinity for the clouds. The family of whooping cranes flies further and further in their search for food. They scour the surrounding prairies, wheat fields and forest edges, always on the lookout for a coyote or pack of wolves.

Where has the summer gone?

The once far flung families begin to gather at Necedah National Wildlife Refuge, a large wetland in the heart of the glacial till of Wisconsin. Nearly three dozen endangered birds, where once there were none, are preparing for their historic flight of 1225 miles to a wetland in south-central Florida.

Most of these birds learned the route from a small, ultra-light aircraft and team of ornithologists who wisely thought to expand the range of the nearly extinct species. In the 1960s and

70s there was only one flock that nested in Northern Canada and spent the winter on the Gulf Coast of Texas. One hurricane could wipe out an entire species. These ornithologists, people who study birds, thought that if they could establish a second flock in their former range it would be insurance against a calamity. Their plan seems to be working!

We are now witnessing the first successful flight of young whooping cranes who are learning the route from their parents, not a plane!

The day has come, a cold, freezing fog hovers above the ground. The older birds, who have made the trip on their own several times, they know, they know that this is the day. This cold wind coming down from Canada will make their journey easier.
It is dawn, do you see the young cranes leaping and whooping it up? They seem to know instinctively it is time. Several whooping cranes take three or four long, strong strides, flapping their wings, striving towards the sky! They flap vociferously. They catch the wind and begin to lift. In the next several moments all of the cranes are in the air. Slowly they circle looking for that thermal, a place where the earth reflects heat and the rising warm air lifts the cranes higher and higher.

The cranes form a large V, with some of the older cranes who best know the way leading the flock. In a V, the lead bird cuts through the wind, like an arrowhead, making it easier for the birds coming behind. When he or she gets tired they fall to the back to rest and let another bird lead. From great heights, the flock can glide rather effortlessly all day. In this way they can cover 100 – 200 miles every day they fly.

They fly over Rockford and Peoria, Illinois. Just south of Peoria, along the Illinois River, in a farmer's field, they find a small pond that is not yet frozen. The flock decides to rest and refuel, taking a couple of days off to regain some strength. Word spreads throughout the community; they get their pictures on the front page of the local papers! Birdwatchers come to oogle them. As long as the people stay far enough away and use their binoculars and spotting scopes to get a closer look, the birds are not bothered by the attention. As long as they do not have to take off and fly away scared at an odd hour so they waste precious fuel, having humans near, but not too near, actually keeps the coyotes and other predators at bay.

After a few days of devouring fish and crawdads, the cranes take flight once more, to southern Illinois, on to Tennessee, through Alabama and Georgia, and eventually they arrive at their winter home in the swamps of Florida.

The winter is mild, unlike last winter when several cranes perished in the cold. This sub-tropical climate is perfect for the young cranes. They whoop and dance practicing for the springtime to come. But all is not well...

Late in the winter, late at night, while the cranes are sleeping, a bobcat stealth-fully stalks the flock. She creeps closer and closer. On padded feet she silently, patiently, crawls the last fifty feet. With a burst of speed she lunges, leaps and grabs a sleeping young crane by the neck. The parents squawk! They attack the bobcat, flapping and pecking, but it is too late. The bobcat shakes her head, snaps the neck of the crane and runs off, carrying the crane away.

Yes, it is sad to watch the death of a creature so rare and so beautiful, but the bobcat has her offspring growing inside of her, and the death of one crane means that several kittens will be born soon, plump and healthy.

Most of the cranes survive the winter with ...

Long legs for stalking in the shallow swamp
A long neck and wings
      for long distant aerodynamic flight and
A long beak for snatching up frogs and fish, snakes and mice.

WHOOOOP! WHOOP! WHOOOOOP! Song of the
>> whooping crane!
They dance when the earth rises,
>> when the snow melt floods the rising creek.
They dance when the pasque flower pushes up through the
>> springing earth.
They dance when the sun rises,
>> when the flocks of birds rise from the trees,
>> rising from the everglades to the great north woods.
In the tall prairie grasses,
>> head bobbing like cattails in a spring storm wings
>> extended, long legs strutting,
>> they dance!

As springtime returns to the far Northwoods, these ancient birds return to their former homelands, return from the brink of extinction, to once again whoop it up on the prairies! Can you look into the future? Do you see the great grand children of these cranes, now in large flocks, making this same migration, season after season? If you can dream it, maybe, we can work together to make it come true.

CRANE POETRY

Here are two of the poems in the story, a haiku, and an acrostic poem. The narrative poem, the last one in the story, is also the outline for this story, which you could turn into the outline for a persuasive essay. Make a list of colorful descriptive phrases about your favorite bird. Use those phrases to play with poetry, experiment with a few different forms, then use those poems to write a story and an essay about your favorite bird.

At first light, a crane
lifts its long legs, wings stretch
singing up the sun

Crane dance
Red head and long tail feathers
A fancy dancer to rival the Lakota
Nearer and nearer his mate, clacking beaks together
Entangled in the dance of love, crane dance

THE WISE QUAIL
A New Twist on an Old Fable

When the pioneers first came to the prairies of Illinois, there were bobwhite quail beyond number. A single hunter with his net could capture 100 per day and ship them off to the gourmet restaurants in Chicago.

A hunter would sneak up on a flock of quail and throw a huge circular net over the feeding birds, catching almost every quail in the flock. Their numbers were quickly depleted. But among the quail was one as wise as Buddha. He quickly devised a plan that would save the quail.

He called the great flocks together and told them, *"When you see the dark cloud circle overhead, do not panic or cry out in fear. Calmly push your head through a hole in the net and all together flap your wings. Together we can lift the net and fly to safety. Then land in a small bush or tree and the net will tangle in its branches allowing all of you to escape harm. Remember, it is not through panic and quarreling that we succeed. It is only when we work together as a team."*

The next time a hunter threw a net, the dark cloud sent a shiver of fear through the flock, but one bird whistled and reminded the others. They all poked their head through the net and flapping together, they all flew away to safety. For weeks the hunters' nets were empty.

But then one morning as a young quail landed among his flock he accidentally landed on the wing of another bird. The two began arguing and whistling loudly. This attracted a hunter who threw his net capturing the quarreling birds. The worst tragedy was that many other quail were also captured with these two quarreling birds.

The quail soon learned that teamwork can solve many problems. And to this day, hunters no longer use nets to hunt quail. Oh, and the name of that wise quail from so long ago, the other quail still call out his name whenever there is danger, you know… Bob White, bobwhite, bobwhite.

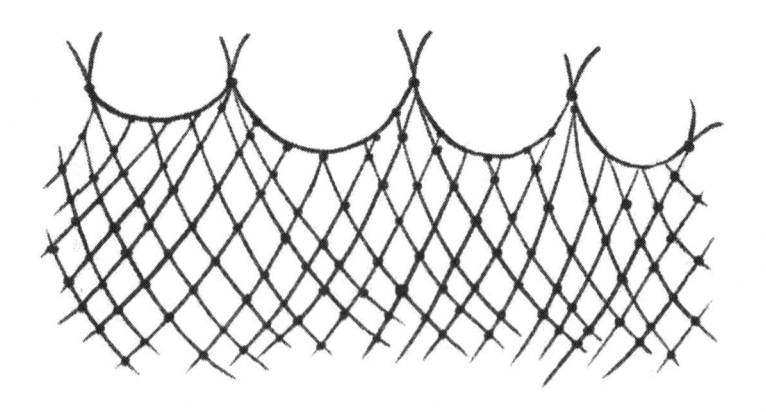

JUMPING MOUSE
A Lakota Story Adapted Into a Play You Can Perform

CHARACTERS:
(Masks can be made with paper plates and construction paper. Scripts can be taped inside the masks.)
Narrator – Tells the story and helps stitch things together.
Jumping Mouse – A little mouse on a journey to being an eagle.
Village of Mice/Chorus – Happy to stay put, sing often, parts for many.
Younger Mouse – Never heard the sound before.
Older Mouse – Heard the sound once and ignored it.
Raccoon – A guide on the Trail of Life.
Frog – One who lives in two worlds.
Wise One – A false prophet.
Buffalo – Giver of life.
Wolf – Guide to the Sacred Mountains.
Eagle – What we all strive to be!

SETTING:
The prairies, rivers edge and mountains of America. This could be a series of simple back drops painted on butcher paper. You could also add a few rocks and potted flowers to the foreground and a large sheet of blue paper as both the river and medicine lake.

The play opens with the village mice scurrying about, running here and there gathering seeds, making little nests from grass. The narrator standing stage right the entire time begins:

NARRATOR: Many long winters ago, there was a little mouse, a lot like many other little mice, who was always busy, running here and there, doing this and that, but whenever he was quiet *(Scurrying mice freeze.)* and still, Shh!, he would hear this roaring sound deep within. He asked another little mouse,

JUMPING MOUSE: "Have you ever heard that sound before?"

YOUNGER MOUSE: "What sound? Oh, I guess I never stopped to listen before."

NARRATOR: And she disappeared into a hole in a cottonwood tree. She wasn't much help. So my friend the little mouse asked an older mouse,

JUMPING MOUSE: "Have you ever heard that sound before?"

OLDER MOUSE: "Ah, yes, I heard it once. I just ignored it and it went away. If you keep busy then you won't notice." (Mice begin scurrying about once again.)

NARRATOR: So my little friend tried to ignore this sound. As long as he was busy, running here and there, doing this and that he did not hear it, but whenever he was quiet, *(Scurrying mice freeze.)* Shh!, he would hear that sound, a still, quiet voice, a roaring sound far away. One day he decided to investigate.

JUMPING MOUSE: "I want to know what that sound is and where it is coming from…"

(The chorus/village mice are always on stage. When they are not front and center they fade into neat rows towards the back acting like an ancient Greek Choir.)

NARRATOR: So he decided to head away from the safety of his village towards where he thought the sound was coming from. *(Speaking to the audience),* Please indulge me, imagine you are this little mouse. Please put your fingers together like this, *(Weave fingers together.)* and put them over your eyes. This is all a little mouse knows, what is right in front of his nose. If you turn your fingers out like whiskers, this is what a mouse sees, what is within his whiskers reach. Now you can put your fingers down, you look pretty silly! But this is the world of a mouse. Imagine you are this little mouse heading down a trail you have never been down before.

JUMPING MOUSE: *(Sniff, sniff)* "There are things to smell I have never smelled before. M-m-m, there are things to eat I have never tasted before." *(As he is walking around he is surprised by the raccoon.)*

RACCOON: "Hello little brother. Where are you going?"

JUMPING MOUSE: *(Startled)* "Oh, who are you?"

RACCOON: "Don't be afraid. I am your old friend raccoon. Where are you going?"

JUMPING MOUSE: "Well, I hear this roaring in my ears and I want to know what it is and where it is coming from."

RACCOON: "Ah, what you hear is the river, the river of life. Would you like me to take you there?"

JUMPING MOUSE: *(Thinking aloud)* "If the raccoon goes with me he could act as guide and be a witness. He could tell the other mice about this thing called a river." *(Turning to the raccoon)* "Yes, yes, please, I would be so grateful."

NARRATOR: The raccoon took the paw of the little mouse and guided him down to the river.

Now imagine again that you are this little mouse and you are standing next to this huge river. Like the Illinois or Mississippi River. In some places there were white water rapids. In other places there were still deep pools. But this was no ordinary river, this was the River, the River of Life. All of life was reflected here. All of life came to refresh themselves in these waters.

Soon they came to a shallow place with duckweeds, lily pads and cattails.

RACCOON: Let me introduce you to a friend of mine, the frog.

FROG: "Bur-r-r-rump, Bur-r-r-rump. Would you like some medicine powers?"

JUMPING MOUSE: "Sure, What do I have to do?"

FROG: "Squat down r-r-real low."

(So the little mouse squats down as low as he can and jumps on cue.)

FROG: "And JUMP!"

NARRATOR: The little mouse jumped as high as he could. And for the first time in his life he could see beyond his whiskers. He saw the sacred mountains and SPLASH! He landed in the river.

JUMPING MOUSE: "You tricked me! You tricked me!"

FROG: "Are you alright?"

JUMPING MOUSE: "Yes. I guess so..."

FROG: "And think about it, now you know the river. Before you had only seen the river, now you have been immersed in the waters of life. And what did you see? "

JUMPING MOUSE: "I saw the mountains! I want to tell my friends about the mountains..." *(confused)* "...but I don't know which way to go..."

FROG: "Just keep the sound of the river behind you and you will find your village." *(As the little mouse scurries away the frog calls out,)* "You have a new name! It is Jumping Mouse!"

NARRATOR: Jumping Mouse ran back to his village and began telling all the mice about the things he saw...

JUMPING MOUSE: "Oh you won't believe what I saw, a raccoon and the river, the frog and the mountains..."

VILLAGE MICE: *(Rudely interrupting as if they did not want to listen and were afraid of him. The village mice circle dance around Jumping Mouse. Each of them take turns saying one of these lines.)*
"Look at him."
"He is all wet."
"Why is he wet?"
"It has not rained in several days."
"Maybe he is wet with the saliva of an animal that caught him but he managed to escape."
"Uh, Oh! This means that the animal is still out there!"
"It is still hungry!"
"It might try to eat US!"

(As if transformed to young mice the village mice sit in a circle listening as Jumping Mouse pantomimes telling a story while the narrator speaks.)

NARRATOR: They were afraid and would not listen. But the little mice loved to listen to his stories. He often visited with the raccoon and the frog. He loved to jump, jump, jump and see the mountains. One day the mountains seemed to call to him and he knew he had to go. He told his friends…

JUMPING MOUSE: "I am going to the sacred mountains."

(This time the village mice circle in the opposite direction.)

VILLAGE MICE:
"Do not leave the safety of the village!"
"Do not go! No don't go!"
"Why would you want to leave the warmth of your village? You know that out there are hawks and eagles out there. They are waiting to swoop down and eat you!"

NARRATOR: This was not what Jumping Mouse wanted to hear, but he knew he had to go, so he bid a due and off he went. Jumping Mouse ran and ran across the wide open prairie.

(The village mice fade to the back of the stage in neat rows. Whenever Jumping Mouse is running the choir sings: Hey-Nickity Hey-wanna Hey-Nickity, Hey-wanna, Asay-wanna, hey-wanna, asa-wanna. Whenever the narrator talks about running. Jumping mouse pantomimes running, running in place.)

Out of breathe he came into the shade of an ancient sage bush. There in the shade of the sage he could rest. M-m-m-m, he found some new seeds he had never eaten before. Oh, there were soft strong cord grasses growing there that would make a fine home for his family. He could live here contentedly the rest of his days… but no, the spirit of the mountains called him on.

As he explored he soon found an old mouse who looked wise and venerable. Jumping Mouse was embarrassed by his youth and didn't know what to say.

JUMPING MOUSE: "Uh, hello, my name is Jumping Mouse, um, who are you?"

WISE ONE: "I am the old one, the wise one. I have lived alone so long I have forgotten my name. You can call me the wise one."

JUMPING MOUSE: "Oh, do you know the animals of the prairie?"

WISE ONE: "I know their names, buffalo, prairie dog, owl. I know their names and that is good enough!"

JUMPING MOUSE: *(Talking to the audience as if he is thinking aloud.)* "Even I know that if you only know someone's name you do not truly know them. I do not want to seem disrespectful, but I am beginning to doubt the wisdom of this old one. Let me give him a little test." *(Turning to the Wise One, politely ask),* "Do you know about the sacred mountains?"

WISE ONE: *(With a dismissive tone.)* "Ah, yes. I have heard of the mountains, but this is just a myth, a story the old ones tell their children, but it is not true. The mountains are not real. Do not believe."

JUMPING MOUSE: *(Thinking aloud, to audience)* "I have seen the mountains with my own eyes. I know they are real." *(Turning to Wise One)* "Thank you, thank you for your kindness and hospitality, but I need to go. I am going to those mountains."

WISE ONE: *(The tone changes to a bitter, harsh warning.)* "Do not go! You know that out there are hawks and eagles waiting to swoop down and eat you!"

NARRATOR: This was not what Jumping Mouse wanted to be reminded of, but he knew he had to go, so he bid a due and off he went.

(Whenever Jumping Mouse is running the choir sings: "Hey-Nickity, Hey-wanna, Hey-Nickity, Hey-wanna, Asay-wanna, hey-wanna, asa-wanna, hey-wanna." Jumping Mouse pantomimes running, running in place. Wise One fades off stage left as Buffalo comes on stage, stage.)

NARRATOR: Well, Jumping Mouse ran and ran across the wide open prairie. He dodged and darted, looking up, trying not to get eaten. Finally, out of breath he came into the shade of a choke cherry tree.

Have you eaten a choke cherry? They are sweet and tart. Like sucking on a lemon they make you pucker up and dry out your mouth, *(mumbling)*, but they are juicy, so you eat another but soon you can hardly talk…

M-m-m. He also found that inside the fruit, the seed was like a nut. And under the shade of this tree grew bunch grass, called bunch grass because it grows in big bunches. When Jumping Mouse crawled inside he pushed some of the grass aside and found it was the biggest lodge he could imagine. His extended family could move in and live comfortably, everything a little mouse could ever want. He could live here the rest of days...but no... the mountains called him on.

BUFFALO: *(Begin wheezing and moaning.)*

NARRATOR: As Jumping Mouse explored the shade of this choke cherry he found a huge mound of brown fur, going up and down.

BUFFALO: *(Wheeze and moan, cough.)*

JUMPING MOUSE: "Oh, no something is terribly wrong with this beautiful creature. Is there anything I can do to help?"

BUFFALO: *(Wheeze and cough throughout).* "There is nothing you can do for me. I am very sick and afraid I might die. If I die, I fear the people shall die, too, for my flesh is their food. My bones make their tools. My fur makes their clothes and covers their lodges. But there is nothing you can do. The medicine woman says only the eye of a mouse can heal me and I do not know what a mouse is..."

JUMPING MOUSE: *(hesitant, quietly to himself)* "I, I am a mouse, I, I have two eyes."

NARRATOR: Now mind you he did not say this, but went off under the choke cherry to think about it. Let me ask, how many of you, when faced with a dilemma will sometimes go off by yourself and sit quietly? As soon as he was quiet he heard that still voice inside, and it said, "You are a mouse. You have two eyes. You can not let her die, and the people die, too?" Jumping Mouse went back to the buffalo and said,

JUMPING MOUSE: "I am a mouse. Let me give you my eye." *(Make the motion as if his eye flew out of his head and into the buffalo. Cover the eye.)*

BUFFALO: *(Jump up and begin pawing the earth and snorting.)* "I am made whole!" *(She looks down at the mouse),* "Little brother! What you have done?! But you are in luck because now a part of you is a part of me and I know your story. And you are in luck. I can take you to the foot of the mountains. Run underneath me and I will protect you from the hawks and eagles."

JUMPING MOUSE: *(With one eye closed.)* "This is great! Much more than I bargained for!" *He gets in under the buffalo and they pantomime running. Jumping Mouse is running and the choir sings: Hey-Nickity, Hey-wanna Hey-Nickity, Hey-wanna, Asay-wanna, hey-wanna, asa-wanna.)*

NARRATOR: Once again, imagine you are this little mouse. Now you are running under a buffalo with one eye watching four legs. A buffalo can weigh more than a ton, 2000 pounds. Every time a hoof hit the ground it was like a little earthquake.

Jumping Mouse ran and ran watching for the four legs with his one eye, until finally they came to the foot of the mountains and buffalo said,

BUFFALO: "I cannot go any further. I am an animal of the prairie. If I try to climb these mountains I am afraid I might fall and we would both be hurt."

JUMPING MOUSE: "Oh, thanks for bringing me this far. I must admit that I was afraid."

BUFFALO: "You had no reason to fear, because my way is the Sun Dance Way and I know where every foot must go, but I must go. Before I leave, let me introduce you to a friend of mine, Brother Wolf." *(Buffalo fades off stage left as wolf comes on stage.)*

WOLF: *(Confused, psychotic scream!)* "Ah! Are you a wolf? I'm scared of wolves! I don't like wolves. Oh, yeah, that's right. I am a wolf... ha, ha, ha, I forget sometimes. Are you a wolf?"

JUMPING MOUSE: *(Thinking aloud, to audience)* "Something is seriously wrong with this guy, such a beautiful animal." (Turning to the wolf) "Brother wolf ..."

WOLF: *(Confused, psychotic scream!)* "Ah! Are you a wolf? I'm scared of wolves! I don't like wolves. Oh, yeah, that's right. I am a wolf... ha, ha, ha, I forget sometimes. Are you a wolf?"

JUMPING MOUSE: *(Thinking aloud, to audience)* "There must be something I can do to help ..."

NARRATOR: Again, Jumping Mouse went off by himself to think. As soon as he was quiet, he heard that still, small voice... "Your eyes. They seem to have some magical power. Give him your eye." Jumping Mouse went back to the wolf and said,

JUMPING MOUSE: "Brother wolf..."

WOLF: "AHH!"

JUMPING MOUSE: "No, calm down. Let me give you my eye." *(Act as though his other eye flies from his head and into the wolf Close both eyes.)*

WOLF: "I am made whole!" *(Startled, looking down at mouse.)* "Oh, little brother, what you have done? But you are in luck, because now a part of you is a part of me and I know your story. You are in luck. I am the guide to the sacred mountains and I can take you to the top."

NARRATOR: The little mouse put his paw in the paw of the mighty wolf and the wolf guided him up the steep slope. *(Pantomime climbing. The choir sings a wolf song: Whoa-Whoa-Whoa-Whoa-Whoa-Whoa-Whoa - Yeah-Yeah-yeah-yeah-yeah-yeah-yeah.)*

Finally they came to the top of the mountain where there was a small glacial lake. But this was no ordinary lake, this was the place where all life began and all of the creatures of the mountains came here to drink. The people came here every spring to honor the beginning time. Wolf described all and said,

WOLF: "I must leave you here, for there are others who wish to climb these mountains and I am their guide. But before I go, let me introduce you to a friend of mine."

FROG: "Bur-r-r-rump, Bur-r-r-rump. Would you like some medicine powers?"

JUMPING MOUSE: "Sure, what do I have to do?"

FROG: "Squat down r-r-real low..." *(The little mouse squats down as low as he can, and pauses before he jumps.)* "And JUMP!"

NARRATOR: Just as Jumping Mouse was about to leap he heard the sound of the wind ... no, it was the sound of wings. He jumped. It hit! The little mouse jumped as high as he could, but he did not fall! And he could see! It was blurry at first, but he could see like he had never seen before. He could see colors. *(Pantomime flying.)* And the wind carried him higher and higher. He could see his village and the river. He could see the prairie fire racing over the horizon. He could see the buffalo and the mountain. He could see the wolf and the lake. At the edge of the lake he saw the frog who said,

FROG: "You have a new name … It is … Eagle!"

(The village mice begin to sing as the Eagle dances in a circle. Everyone falls in behind and everyone joins in an eagle dance.)

Call and response, the narrator sings and everyone repeats:

NARRATOR:	**CHORUS:**
We all fly like eagles	We all fly like eagles
flying so high	flying so high
circling the universe	circling the universe
on wings of pure light	on wings of pure light
Oh itchi-ti-ti,	Oh itchi-ti-ti,
Itchi-ti-oh,	Itchi-ti-oh,
Oh itchi-ti-ti,	Oh itchi-ti-ti,
Itchi-ti-oh,	Itchi-ti-oh,

THE BITTERN AND THE MUSSEL
An Chinese Fable

A little brown heron, a least bittern, was wading along the edge of a river when he came across a large river clam, or mussel. The bittern was hungry and poked his greedy beak into the mussel's shell. The mussel felt the intrusion and quickly clamped his shell shut, squeezing the beak of the bittern.

This bittern was stubborn and would not pull his beak out of the mussel. This mussel was determined and would not relax his grip for fear that the bittern would eat him.

The bittern muttered, *"If you do let go of my beak, today, tomorrow or next week, soon you will die and soon you will reek!"*

The mussel responded, *"If you do not remove your beak, today, tomorrow or next week, soon you will die and soon you will reek!"*

But the bittern was stubborn. The mussel was determined. The two of them were bound in an eternal struggle... that is, they were bound together until a fox spied the struggle. He ended the dispute by eating them both!

SNOW BUNTINGS' LULLABY
A Siberian Folktale

Where I live in Northern Illinois, we have very cold winters. The entire month of January is often below freezing with a week or more below zero. There is a lot of snow. So no one is surprised to know that many of our birds migrate south for the winter. But I was delightfully surprised to learn that a number of birds fly south from the Arctic Circle to Northern Illinois and spend their winters in the forests and farm fields near me! When there is a deep snow pack up north we will see snowy owls. And every winter we see horned larks, longspurs and snow buntings feeding in the corn fields. I especially like snow buntings, so when I found this story I had to learn it and tell it to you!

In the far northern reaches of Siberia, Alaska, Greenland and Canada, there is a small, sparrow-sized bird that has a most delightful song. Because there are no trees in the tundra they build their nests on the ground. They will make their nests out of moss, dried grasses, feather and reindeer fur. They hide their nest in a crack between rocks and their tiny eggs looked like speckled rocks.

One young pair of snow buntings was about to raise their first brood of babies. Can you imagine their excitement when the little eggs began to shake? A little crackling sound was made. A crack appeared and the first little beak poked out. Soon all of the eggs were crackling and popping open. The new mother and father were so proud of their babies. But as soon as the babies popped out of their shells they began to cry! *"Cheep! Cheep! Cheep! Cheep!"*

"Oh, Pappa, Pappa, what are we going to do?" asked Momma Snow Bunting.

Pappa said, *"Here is a little song my momma used to sing with me:"* (Listen the first time)

"Whose little toes are these?
Whose little wings are these?
Whose little beak is this?
Go to sleep."

And the baby snow buntings went to sleep!

"Oh, Pappa, that is a sweet little song, please teach it to me," said Momma Snow Bunting. And so he did.

Pappa said, *"Now I must go and get some food, because we know those babies will be hungry when they wake up."*

Pappa flew away. Watching this whole time was Karoak the Raven. Raven waited until Pappa snow bunting flew away. Then he flew down and said, *"I like that song! Karoak! I want that song! Karoak! Give me that song right now or else! Ar-Ar-Ar-Ar-Ar..."*

"No, no," said Momma Snow Bunting, *"That song is ours, I cannot give it to you."*

But Raven was making so much racket that he woke up the baby snow buntings. And they began to cry, *"Cheep! Cheep! Cheep! Cheep!"* So Momma began to sing,

"Whose little toes are these?
Whose little wings are these?
Whose little beak is this?
Go to sleep."

As the last little bit of music came streaming from her beak, Raven swooped down and stole it. He stole the song!

The babies woke up and started to cry, *"Cheep! Cheep! Cheep! Cheep!"* Momma tried to sing, but nothing came out. The babies kept crying, *"Cheep! Cheep! Cheep! Cheep!"* OH, it was driving Momma Snow Bunting crazy!

Just then Pappa Snow Bunting came back. *"Momma, Momma, why are the babies crying? Did you not sing our song for them?"*

Poppa could hardly understand what Momma was saying,,

she was crying herself. "Pappa, Raven stole our song, and I cannot get the babies to stop crying." Pappa fed the babies and that helped a great deal. They stopped crying.

Then Pappa Snow Bunting flew over to the cliff edge where Raven had his nest. *"Raven, give me back my song! I learned it from my momma. It is our song and it is not right for you to steal it!"*

Raven laughed,*"Karoak! It is my song now! Ar-Ar-Ar!"* Raven's babies woke up so Raven started to sing in a croaking voice,

"Whose little toes are these?
Whose little wings are these?
Whose little beak is this?
Go to sleep."

As the last little bit of melody came from Raven's beak, Pappa Snow Bunting flew up and grabbed that ribbon of song and flew back to his nest. The baby snow buntings were waking up, so Momma and Pappa sang together: (Do you want to sing-a-long?)

"Whose little toes are these?
Whose little wings are these?
Whose little beak is this?
Go to sleep."

And so they did… good night baby snow buntings…

MEADOWLARK

A meadowlark sings
a glorious trill
from the top of a gnarled tree.
His warbling voice
his ecstatic song
is brighter than the sun.
The stars fade in comparison.
The sun rises with his beckoning,
the prairie blazes with his melody
and my heart catches this fire
with this love for this life
this day
this infinite moment…
…of glorious song.

WRITE YOUR OWN BIRD TALES

What is your favorite wild bird?

Draw a picture of this bird in its natural habitat. Add a nest, eggs, and a picture of its young. Draw the differences between the male and female of this species.

On a separate sheet of paper, answer as many of these questions as you can: What does it look like? What are the different colors of male and female birds? Where does it live? Nest? Feed? Migrate? What does it do? How does it feed? Attract a mate? Tend its nest? Raise its young? What are its enemies? How does it survive? What does it do in each season? What is its role in the ecosystem? For the questions you cannot answer, either look them up in a book, surf the web, or better yet go outside and observe the bird to learn directly from your favorite bird! Imagine making an annual migration. Write a story or poem about the perils of the trip and the adventures you would have along the way.

John James Audubon spent many months living in the wildest places in America studying and drawing birds. Spend some time each day over the next few weeks collecting data about your favorite bird. Observe it at different times of day and take notes on its behavior. Ask yourself questions and then look for answers. What are your theories about what you observe? Keep a journal of your observations always noting the time, temperature and any weather conditions. How does weather affect behavior?

Use this information to write a biography of your favorite bird describing its life from egg to wing.

Read About Audubon's Birds:

Visit The National Audubon Society to learn more about Audubon and to read some of his essays:
http://www.audubon.org/birds-of-america

Study the Birds at your feeders:

Put different kinds of bird feeders outside your classroom or living room window. Fill each feeder with a different kind of food. Keep a bird book next to the window with a clipboard and pencil. Make a chart so you can keep track of how many different types of birds come to your feeder and how many of each species. Keep notes on which types of birds prefer which types of seeds. Compare your charts over time to see which birds are seasonal visitors and which are year-round residents.

Each year Cornell Labs conducts a bird feeder study and you can help scientists track long term population trends by sending your data to: http://feederwatch.org

Follow Bird Migrations:

Audubon was also the first scientist in America to band a bird. He put a small silver thread on the ankle of a phoebe before it left in the fall to see if it returned in the spring. It did.

Use the map on the next page to chart bird migrations. Draw a line from the nesting grounds to the winter home. Use a different color for each bird.

Bald Eagle: Nest in Canada, winters in the Mississippi Valley.
Veery: Nest in Delaware, winters along the Amazon River.
Ruby Throated Hummingbird: Nest in Illinois and winters in the Yucatan.
Whooping Crane: Nest in Northern Canadian Rockies, winters on the Gulf Coast.
Snow Bunting: Nest in the Arctic Circle and spend the winter in farm fields from Montana to Illinois.

Add your favorite bird to this map and begin to keep track of which birds pass through your neighborhood and where they are traveling to or from. For more information about migration and to help with global monitoring, check out:
www.learner.org/jnorth/

ABOUT THE STORIES & THEIR SOURCES:

- "The Sun's Symphony" first appeared in my book of poetry, Singing Up the Sun, (Fox Tales International 2010)
- "How Birds Got their Feathers," - I heard told by Joe Bruchac, and it is in his book Iroquois Stories (Crossing Press 1985)
- "The Squirrel and the Thrush" is by Ivan Andreyevich Krylov, 1809.
- "Hummingbird Places the Stars" - I learned at camp 40 years ago.
- "Hummingbird's Ruby Throat" is loosely based on a story from Tales From Silver Lands (Doubleday 1924).
- "Hummingbird and Crane" was collected by James Mooney more than 100 years ago, but my favorite version is by Jean Starr in Tales From the Cherokee Hills, (James Blair, 1988)
- "The Crane Maiden" is found in several children's books, including Crane Wife by Odds Bodkins (Harcourt 1998) and "The Crane Maiden" by Miyoko Matsutani (Parents Magazine Press 1968)
- "Lord of the Cranes" is based on old Taoist legend and published by Kerstin Chen (North-South Books 2000)
- "The Whooping Cranes' Migration" and "Crane Poetry" first appeared in my book, Content Area Reading, Writing and Storytelling (Teacher Ideas Press 2009).
- "The Wise Quail" is my adaptation of one of Tolstoy's Fables.
- "Jumping Mouse" is a traditional Lakota Story.
- "The Bittern and the Mussel" is a Chinese fable from Frederic Cooper's An Argosy of Fables (Stokes 1921)
- "The Snow Buntings' Lullaby" is from Margaret Read MacDonald's Tuck-Me-In Tales (August House, 1996), retold from Kutkha the Raven: Animal Stories of the North by Fainna Solaska (Moscow: Malysh Publishers, 1981)
- "The Meadowlark" is also from my book, Singing Up the Sun.

Brian "Fox" Ellis is an internationally acclaimed author, storyteller, historian, and naturalist. He has worked with The Abraham Lincoln Presidential Library and Museum, The Field Museum and dozens of other museums across the country. He has hosted, produced written and researched several documentaries for PBS and has recently launched a podcast, "Fox Tales International." He is the author of more than 2 dozen books including the critically acclaimed <u>Learning From the Land: Teaching Ecology Through Stories and Activities</u>, (Libraries Unlimited, 2011), a series of Chautauqua style autobiographies, <u>History In Person</u> series, and this collection of Fox Tales Folklore. Many of his stories are also available on his YouTube channel, "Fox Tales International." He and his wife run a Bed and Breakfast in Bishop Hill, Illinois, The Twinflower Inn, where he also leads bird watching adventures!

Devin McSherry is a freelance illustrator, hand-lettering artist, and surface pattern designer born and raised in the Prairie State of Illinois. Her best days are spent walking through nature, illustrating things that inspire her, cooking from scratch, and keeping her hands busy with sewing and other crafts. She's also learning to garden and enjoys getting involved with local permaculture-focused organinzations. She currently lives alongside her husband, Ryan, in the suburbs of Chicago. Are you interested in working with Devin on your next creative project? You can view more of her work and get in touch by visiting her website (<u>www.devinmcsherry.com</u>) and following her on Instagram (@devin.mcsherry).

This Book is part of a Multimedia Series Available at
www.foxtalesint.com
Visit this website to see the other books in the series.

If you purchased the audio book
and video here is your access code:

To watch a performance and listen to more
Fox Tales Folklore
in this series you can also subscribe to
the YouTube channel and podcast:

Fox Tales International

Made in the USA
Middletown, DE
06 February 2025